파랑새
BLUEBIRD

창조문학사

파랑새
BLUEBIRD

EUN HEE PAK
박은희 한영시집

Translated from Korean
by Sara Pak
번역: 박사라

Korean Expatriate Literature
California, USA & Seoul, South Korea
&
Cross-Cultural Communications
New York, USA
2019

Copyright © 2019 by Eun Hee Pak

All rights reserved. No part of this book may be used or reproduced in any manner whatsoever without written permissions, except in the case of brief quotations embodied in critical articles and reviews.

Co-published by Korean Expatriate Literature and Cross-Cultural Communications

First Edition, 2019

Library of Congress Control Number: 2019941015

ISBN 978-0-89304-664-4

First printing of Bilingual Edition: 2019

Korean Bilingual Poetry Series #7

Co-publisher: Korean Expatriate Literature
11533 E. Promenade Dr.
Santa Fe Springs, CA 90670 USA
Tel: (562) 929-2338
E-mail: ychopoet@yahoo.com
www.hewemunhak.com

Co-publisher: Cross-Cultural Communications
239 Wynsum Avenue
Merrick, NY 11566-4725 USA
Tel: (516) 868-5635/Fax: (516) 379-1901
E-mail: cccpoetry@aol.com
www.cross-culturalcommunications.com

Printed by Changjo Munhak
86 Gajwaro, Seodaemun-gu,
Dongchun Academy # 5th
Seoul, Korea
Tel: 02-374-9011
E-mail: hmpo@hanmail.net
Cover design by Sara Pak
Cover art (Fabergé egg) by Eun Hee Pak

This book is dedicated to:

My two lovely daughters, husband and other family members.

이 작은 책자를 사랑스러운 나의 두 딸과 남편, 그리고 다른 가족에게 드립니다.

|시인의 말|

　시 「파랑새」는 나에게 특별한 의미가 있지요. 이 시는 나 자신과 내 가족에 대한 사랑과 배려를 그린 시입니다. 이 시로 인해 저는 「해외문인협회」로부터 시인으로 인정받아, 새로운 삶의 영역을 넓혀 갈 수 있는 계기가 되었습니다. 뿐만 아니라, 저에게 새로운 도전에 대한 용기를 북돋아 주었던 시였습니다.
　시 「파랑새」를 계기로 저의 일상생활은 시상을 떠올리고 시를 기록하며 다듬었지요. 그리고 여러 시인들의 아름다운 시집을 읽고 공부하게 되었지요.
　시에 대해 사색하고 배움으로써 저 자신이 좀 더 성숙하고, 성취감과 즐거움을 느낄 수 있었습니다. 한 편 한 편 노트북이 채워갈 때 양심의 마음소리와 말하고 싶었던 삶이 풍요롭게 단축되어 간직 되는 것 같아 깊은 행복을 느끼곤 했지요.
　어느덧 60여 편의 시가 모아졌네요. 남편과 두 딸, 존경하는 시인 조윤호 선생님의 권유로 용기 내어 처녀시집을 내게 되었습니다. 부족해서 두려운 마음이 앞서지만, 저의 마음의 소리를 담은 시들을 책으로 남겨, 사랑하는 두 딸과 그 후손들이 대대로 나의 마음의 글을 읽을 것이라는 기대감에 한 편으로는 보람과 행복함을 느낍니다.
　옆에서 묵묵히 용기와 힘과 사랑을 보내준 남편과 두 딸, 저에게 시를 가르쳐 주시고 옆에서 끊임없이 지도해 주시는 시인 조윤호 선생님께 깊은 감사를 드립니다.

또한 바쁜 회사 일에도 불구하고 엄마의 시들을 손수 본인이 번역하겠다고, 정성과 열성을 다한 둘째 딸 (박사라)에게 감사와 사랑을 전하고 싶습니다. 이 기회를 주신 하느님께도 감사드립니다.
  부족한 시들이지만 저의 시들을 읽고 사색하는 시를 사랑하시는 분들께 조금이나마 행복하고 평화로운 마음이 함께 하길 소망합니다.

―박 은 희

|FOREWORD|

The poem, "Bluebird," written to express my love and care for my family, is special to me. Through this poem, I was officially recognized as a poet in the Korean Expatriate Literary Association. That opened the opportunity for me to expand my scope into the world of poetry. Ultimately, the poem had become my encouragement to embark upon this new exciting challenge.

With this opportunity that "Bluebird" opened, I spent each day creating and revising my poems as I perused and studied the beautiful works of other poets. The sense of growth I obtained while learning from other poets has been fulfilling and most enjoyable. I was greatly happy as I filled my notebook page by page with the thoughts of my conscience and mind wrapped concisely and richly.

Before I knew it, I had somehow gathered 60 poems. Through the encouragement of my husband, my two daughters, and poet Yoon-Ho Cho whom I deeply respect, I mustered my courage to publish my first book of poems. Though I feel some sense of fear and hesitation, given my shortcomings, I also find excitement, fulfillment, and happiness in the thought that my two daughters, whom I love, and future generations will read the sounds of my heart that I preserve within this book.

To my husband and two daughters who steadily gave me encouragement and love, as well as poet Yoon-Ho Cho who taught me poetry and tirelessly coached me, I give my sincerest and deepest appreciation. I wish to send my thanks and love to my second daughter (Sara Pak), who enthusiastically gave it her all in translating my poems despite her busy work schedule. I also thank God for giving me this blessed opportunity.

Though my poems are lacking, I hope that those who love thoughtful poems will read my poetry and, even if a just a little, will feel a happy and peaceful heart together.

― Eun Hee Pak

차례
CONTENTS

시인의 말 | 6
Foreword | 8

1. 새의 노래 A BIRD'S SONG

새의 노래 | 18
A Bird's Song | 19
나의 잔 | 20
My Cup | 21
희망에게 | 22
To Hope | 23
무지개 띠 | 24
Rainbow Band | 25
나의 새벽 | 26
My Dawn | 27
겸손한 솔 잎사귀 | 28
Modest Pine Needles | 29
아버지 목소리 | 30
My Father's Voice | 31
전복 껍질을 보며 | 32
As I See the Abalone Shell | 33

부부 | 34
Married Couple | 35
바위처럼 | 36
Like a Boulder | 37
내가 변하니 | 38
As I Change | 39
작약 꽃 행복 | 40
Peony Flower's Happiness | 41
들꽃처럼 | 42
Like the Wildflower | 43
청소 | 44
Cleaning | 45
모든 것이 시작될 때 | 46
When Everything Begins | 47
침묵 | 48
Silence | 49

2. 해바라기 SUNFLOWER

채송화 닮은 사람 | 52
A Person like Purslane | 53
꽃송이의 가르침 | 54
The Teachings of a Blossom | 55
바다와 작은 새 | 56
The Ocean and the Little Bird | 57
의연한 나무 | 58
Prominent Tree | 59

해바라기 | 60
Sunflower | 61
새벽의 희망 | 62
The Hope of Dawn | 63
달의 모습 | 64
The Moon's Shape | 65
어둠과 침묵 | 66
Darkness and Silence | 67
오른손과 왼손 | 68
Right Hand and Left Hand | 69
행복은 바람 같은 것 | 70
Happiness Is Like the Wind | 71
초봄을 기다리며 | 72
Waiting for Early Spring | 73
자존감이 준 선물 | 74
The Gift From Self-Esteem | 75
봄의 소리 | 76
The Sound of Spring | 77
아보카도 | 78
Avocado | 79
이젠 느낄 수 있어야 하네 | 80
Now It Must Be Felt | 81

3. 파랑새 Bluebird

나의 양식 | 84
My Food | 85

파랑새 | 86

Bluebird | 87

바다 진주 | 88

Ocean Pearl | 89

할머니의 손 | 90

Grandma's Hand | 91

나의 것으로 | 92

To Make Mine | 93

별똥별 쏟아지는 산 | 94

The Shooting Star Mountain | 95

햇볕만 느끼세요 | 96

Feel Only the Sun | 97

명상의 숲 | 98

Meditative Forest | 99

일장춘몽이었다고 | 100

I Have an Empty Fantasy | 101

향기 품은 이슬로 | 102

The Dew That Bore Fragrance | 103

구름처럼 | 104

Like the Cloud | 105

아침을 맞이하며 | 106

As I Welcome the Morning | 107

밤을 맞이하며 | 108

As I Welcome the Night | 109

추억은 | 110

Memories | 111

눈이 오면 | 112
When It Snows | 113
선인장 열매 | 114
The Cactus Fruit | 115

4. 그 손, 그 발 THAT HAND, THAT FOOT

그 손, 그 발 | 118
That Hand, That Foot | 119
마른 꽃으로 | 120
With the Dried Flower | 121
감사와 미안이란 말 | 122
Thank You and Sorry | 123
가을밤에 | 124
On an Autumn Night | 125
은행잎을 보며 | 126
Looking Upon the Gingko Leaf | 127
잡초 | 128
Weeds | 129
산들바람 | 130
Breeze | 131
어제, 오늘, 내일 | 132
Now, Today, Tomorrow | 133
사랑의 힘 | 134
The Strength of Love | 135
어둠속에도 | 136
Even in the Dark | 137

우리 가족 | 138
Our Family | 139
사랑의 딸들 | 140
Daughters of Love | 141
나의 빛, 나의 친구 | 142
My Light, My Friend | 143
싹 | 144
Sprout | 145
빗속의 나의 방 | 146
My Room Within the Rain | 147
선한 눈망울 | 148
Good-natured Eye | 149
- 서평 | 박은희의 시 세계 | 150
- Book Review | 155
- 작가에 관하여 | 161
- About the Author | 162

Hawaiian Beach, Photograph by Pak Family

Part 1

새의 노래
A BIRD'S SONG

새의 노래

삐럭삐럭 피리 부는 새
해질 무렵 황혼 속에서
새의 노래를 들었네.

내가 듣고 있는 새소리를
새는 알지 못하리.
새의 노래를 듣고 있는 한
나는 행복에 젖어 있음을 알아차렸네.

A Bird's Song

A chirping bird plays its vocal flute
In the dusk of sunset time
I listened to the bird's own song.

That I was listening to the bird,
The bird knew not at all.
Whenever I did hear its song
I noticed I was soaked in happiness.

나의 잔

질박하고 투박한 잔
고풍스럽고 우아한 잔
소박한 시골 소녀 같은 잔
과연 난 어떤 잔을 갖고 있을까?

감미로운 향이 풍기는 과일주스 잔
쓴 냄새 풍기는 한약 담긴 잔
가을에 찻집에서 마시던 찻잔
과연 나의 잔은 어느 향이 담겨 있을까?

지나가는 나그네님!
당신은 어떤 잔에
어느 향인가요?

My Cup

An impoverished, rugged cup
A quaint and elegant cup
Another one humble as a country girl
I wonder what kind of cup I hold?

A juice cup sending whiffs of mellow fragrance
Another of bitter smell filled with herbal medicine
A teacup in a teahouse used in autumn time
I wonder what scent my cup contains?

Oh passing traveler!
Which cup and
What fragrance do you hold?

희망에게

불 화마 속에서
달구어진 식칼
평범한 칼은 아니다.

단련하면 할수록
빛을 내는 별 같은 희망
가슴에 차곡차곡 쌓인다는 것.

내가 아는 것은
이것뿐,
무엇을 더 바랄까.

To Hope

Within a fiery urn
The forged kitchen knife
Is no ordinary knife.

The more that one is trained
Hope, like a star that shines with light,
Grows little by little in the heart.

What I know
Is only this,
What more would I want.

무지개 띠

물안개로 엮어진 색실을 모아
하늘에 쏘아 올린
색동 하늘 머리띠.

힘들 때 같이 있어 주겠다는
하늘의 약속
희망의 색깔로 하늘에 피어났네.

찰나의 순간 사라져도
늘 마음 속에 새겨진
내 영혼의 일곱 무지개.

Rainbow Band

Gathering colors mixed up in the mist
Poured out upon the sky
Is a rainbow hairband for the sky.

The sky's promise
To be by your side in troubled times,
The colors of hope have bloomed upon the sky.

Though the moment passes by
My heart always holds
A rainbow, forever mine.

나의 새벽

그대는 초심의 나에게서
멀어진 나를 찾아주는
짙푸른 높은 깃발.

행여 잘못 가던 나의 길
다시 바로 잡아주는
따가운 가르침의 손.

그대는 캄캄한 긴 밤 힘차게 지나
하얀 새날을 만날 수 있게
잠시 쉬며 머무는 정거장.

그대는 영원히
나의 길을 지켜주실
변함없는 나의 스승인 것을.

My Dawn

The first to find myself
That has departed from who I am
Are you, a tall cobalt flag.

That upon the wrong path I walked
You set me back onto the right
Your sharp teaching hand.

You who endured a long, dark night
In order to meet the new white day
You rest a bit at a resting point.

You are forever
The one who will keep me on my path
As you are my unchanging guide.

겸손한 솔 잎사귀

햇볕 욕심에 서로 잎사귀를 넓히던 활엽수
맥없이 가을바람에 퇴색하여 톡톡 떨어지는데

바늘 같은 몸을 줄여 서로 햇볕 양보하던
솔 잎사귀들은 매서운 겨울에도 푸르디푸르네.

겸손함이 솔 향으로 뿜어지니
치유의 초록향이 숲에 가득하네.

따뜻한 흰 눈 이불 옹기종기 나눠덮고
새들의 연초록 봄 연가를 기다리네.

Modest Pine Needles

Greedy for sunlight, the deciduous leaves spread wide open
So easily do they fall at an autumn breeze

But the thin pine needles that conserve to share sunlight
Are ever so green amidst winter so fierce

Modesty sprayed through the pine scent
Fills the forest with a healing green fragrance

Huddled beneath a warm, white snow blanket
Birds wait for the spring sonata to begin.

아버지 목소리

열 손가락으로 햇볕을 가득 담아 가슴에 품고
파도의 흰 거품 속에서
영혼을 꿈꾸며 취할 무렵.

포근한 옛 서울
그 목소리, 그 내음이
파도에 각인 되어
손끝에 저릿하게 도달했네.

타박타박 어린 소녀
다시 걷는 그 골목길
정든 이들의 속삭임 속에
살포시 아버지가 날 부르시네.

뜨거운 모래 위에
따스한 아버지의 정이
맨발에 전해지네.

My Father's Voice

All ten fingers, pulling sunlight into my heart
Cheers to waves of white foam
Does get drunk my dreamy soul.

My tender childhood's Seoul
Its voice, its aroma
Imprinted upon the waves
And did rouse my fingertips.

Pitter patter goes the young girl
Walks again in that small alleyway
Amongst the mutterings of familiar neighbors
My father does call out my name.

And upon the balmy sand,
The heated affection of my father
Is delivered to my bare feet.

전복 껍질을 보며

바위 옆에 붙어 있는
거칠고 까만 전복.

차가운 물보라를 맞고
풍랑과 역경을 겪으며 지켜낸 속껍질.

생을 다하고 나니
비로소 알게 된 전복껍질 속의
무지갯빛 깊은 사랑을

전복을 대하고 있으니
우리 아버지 거친 손이 생각나네.

As I See the Abalone Shell

Attached upon the side of rocks
The rough and blackened abalone

Beat by the frigid ocean spray
Enduring all storm and adversity, it protects the inner shell.

And so does it complete its life.
For the first time, revealed inside the abalone shell
Is a rainbow glisten of deep love

As I see the abalone
I'm reminded of my father's own rough hands.

부부

바람 부는 무도회장에서
낙엽들이 춤을 추는 가을아침
뒤뜰 한쪽에 기대어
마주보는 비와 쓰레받기.

서로의 하는 일과 모양은 달라도
서로 어우러지는
단아하고 온화한 조화.

추위와 무더위 속에서
서로의 온기와 그늘이 되어
쓸어주고, 치워 주며
곰삭아 가는 다정한 하나 같은 둘.

Married Couple

In a windy ballroom
Leaves dance about in an autumn morning,
Leaning in a corner of the yard
The broom and dustpan face each other.

Though each other's shapes and jobs differ,
Their complementing
Sweet and gentle harmony.

In the hot and cold
They become each other's shade and heat
Sweeping and cleaning,
Being worn down fondly, two that are like one.

바위처럼

같은 한자리 지키며
긴 세월이 녹아내린 바위
억세게 비 오면 달게 씻어내고
번개가 치면 때론 반으로
갈라지며 순응하는 바위

바위가 돌이 되고, 모래로 변해도
항시 유용하듯

소리 없이 마음으로 말하는
바위처럼 인생의 그 자리를
침묵으로 지키고 싶습니다.

Like a Boulder

Standing steadfast
The boulder that's polished over ages
In heavy rain, it welcomed the bathing,
Struck by lighting and split in half
The docile rock conforms.

Though the rock becomes two and turns to sand,
It continues to remain useful

Without a sound, only speaking with its heart.
Like a boulder,
I wish to silently fulfill the responsibility of life.

내가 변하니

내가 먼저 변하니
세상의 모진 말들이
수정 은빛 종소리 되고
그 맑은 종소리는
희망의 메아리 되어요.

내가 희망의 메아리가 되니
내 눈에 기울어져 보이던
세상이 바로 섭니다.

As I Change

As I change myself
The world's harsh words
Become crystal silver bell sounds
And the clear bell sounds
Become echoes of hope.

As I adjust to become the echoes of hope
The things that once seemed off to me
Right away are rectified.

작약 꽃 행복

아기 볼 빛 마냥 소담히 얼굴 내민 작약
황홀한 자태 속에
보름달이 뜨네.

오랜 기다린 후 봉오리는 안개 되어
분홍빛 웃음으로 인사 건네고
파시시 떨며 봄 향기를 흘리네.

며칠 후 꽃잎이 웃으며
툭툭 떨어지며 남기는 말
"피어있는 내내 행복했습니다."

피어있는 우리들의 삶도
내내 감사의 꽃을 피웠으면

Peony Flower's Happiness

The peony peeks out its baby cheek-like face
Within its deeply wrapped stance,
There rises a full moon.

After patient waiting, the bulb becomes fog
And with a pink-toned laughter it bows,
Fluttering off the smell of spring.

A few days later as the petals smile
They drop one by one, as they bid farewell as so,
"I was happy while I bloomed".

For our blooming life as well,
May it be a blooming flower of thanks.

들꽃처럼

뿌리내릴 만큼의 소박한 자리에서
하늘이 주는 단 이슬 마시며
가냘프게 자라는 들꽃.

혼자서도 지나는 이에게
늘 평온한 미소
나누어 주는 선한 들꽃.

언제 꺾어질 줄 모르는
변화에도 당당함으로
의연히 감사로 피어있네.

들꽃처럼 아무것도
바라지 않고 하늘만 보고 있어도
맑은 햇살 꿈꾸는
넉넉한 마음 갖고 싶네.

Like the Wildflower

In the modest space where it plants its roots
Gulping heaven's dew
Does grow so well the wildflower.

To those who walk alone
Always peaceful, joyful music
The kind wildflower shares.

Not knowing when it may be broken
Confident in the face of change
Bloomed it has, out of thanksgiving.

Like the wildflower, without expectations
And solely looking up to the sky
Dreaming of the brilliant sunlight
I wish for a generous heart.

청소

가정의 구석 안에
노화 된 먼지
깨끗이 닦아 냈다.

맑은 물에서 흘려보내는
내 오래된 회색 먼지들.

달콤한 여름 향기 머금고
풋내 나는 흰 희망으로
다시 태어나는 오늘.

나의 설레는 마음을
하늘의 빛에 담가 씻은 후
연 파랑 하늘을 담아낸다.

Cleaning

Within the corners of the home
Aged dust
Is cleanly brushed away.

Washing away in clear fresh water
My antiquated grey dust.

Faded in sweet summer scent
Through white hope smelling of fresh cut grass,
A newly born today.

With my fluttering heart
Soaked and bathed with the sky's light,
I capture the light blue sky.

모든 것이 시작될 때

아기의 눈망울이 처음 나를 볼 때
붉은 태양이 하루를 여는 순간
우린 잠시 할 말을 잃습니다.

가슴 뛰는 기쁨의 만남에
진리의 불덩이가 가슴 안으로
물 위에 동그라미 그리며 번집니다.

모든 것이 시작되는 이 순간
알이 부화하듯 깨우치는
겸허한 희망의 기도와
어리석은 마음이여

When Everything Begins

When a baby's pupil first lays eyes on me
The moment the fiery sun opens the day
We in awe are at a loss of words.

In the happiness that meets an excited heart
The fire of truth splashes into the heart
Rippling upon the water on which it draws a circle.

In the moment everything begins
As an egg hatches and awakens
There exists a humble hopeful prayer
And a naive heart.

침묵

이 세상엔
진리로 말하는 것보다
더 큰 기쁨은 없다네.

당신과 나누는 말보다
더 큰 행복은
나도 찾지 못했지.

허공을 떠도는
사랑이란 말도
마음에 상처를 입힌다네.

격려를 내세운 말도
침묵하는 것보다
더 아플 때도 있으니까.

Silence

In this world
It is said there is no happiness
Greater than truthful speaking.

A happiness greater
Than speaking with you
I have not found.

Thrown in the air
Empty words of love
Can dress wounds upon the heart.

Even words of encouragement
Can, even more than silence,
Be painful at times.

Peony Flower, Photograph by Pak Family

Part 2

해바라기
SUNFLOWER

채송화 닮은 사람

채송화 앞에 서면
고개 숙여 보게 된다.

초록빛 나무의 푸른 그림자 사이로
낮아지는 내 모습.

가끔 겸손하여
낮추는 이들 중에

나도 함께 서서
채송화를 바라보네.

A Person like Purslane

When standing in front of a purslane
One's head bows down.

Into the green shadows of the trees
Hides my lowered body.

Among those who at times
Lower themselves in humility,

I stand with them
And look upon the purslanes.

꽃송이의 가르침

나뭇가지에
작은 꽃도
아름답게 피어 있네.

그 작은 꽃도
꽃잎마다
작은 향을 풍기네.

꽃은 작아도
우리에게
아름다움만 주고 가네.

The Teachings of a Blossom

Upon a branch
A small flower
So beautifully has blossomed too.

Even such a tiny flower
Per petal that it has
Gives off a small aroma.

Though little is the blossom,
To us does it give
Beauty and only that.

바다와 작은 새

하얀 이 드러내고
온몸으로
웃음 쏟아내는 바다.

흰 머리 풀어 헤치고 지휘하며
천상의 곡 만들어 내는 바다.

기쁨, 슬픔, 감성을 솔직하게
밸런스를 드러내는 바다는

평화와 안정을
늘 품고 있네.

그 모습을 작은 새는
숨김없이 그대로 배우고 있네.

The Ocean and the Little Bird

Showing white teeth
With its whole body
The ocean pours out its laughter.

With its white hair let loose, running and leading
A heavenly song the ocean does.

Happiness and sadness, honestly
Balancing all exposed emotions.

The ocean always holds.
Peace and security.

Exactly as the ocean shows, the little bird
Without hiding learns just as so.

의연한 나무

의연한 나무는 때가오면
붉고 노란 외출복 준비해
정든 잎사귀들에게 갈아입히지.

순응하며 떨어지는 잎사귀에다
바람 따라 떠오른 얼굴을 담아
그리움의 이야기책들을 나무 밑에 쌓아놓네.

매서운 겨울바람
이야기 책 거름 삼은 나무는
온기품은 연한 바람타고
봉긋, 연초록 배냇저고리 입은
새 순에 사랑을 다시 틔웁니다.

Prominent Tree

When it comes time, the prominent tree
Prepares its red and yellow clothes
And dresses each of its beloved leaves.

Upon the obediently falling leaves
With the wind, faces that are recalled are stored
And below the tree piles up nostalgic storybooks.

Past the bitter winter wind
The tree that by the storybooks was fertilized
Riding the gentle wind that carries warmth
Buds dressed in light green infant's clothes
Sprouts the new bud's love once more.

해바라기

해만 사모하고 살아가는
해바라기.

나도 당신만 바라보고 살 수 없을까?
아무것도 보지 않고
오직 해만 바라보는
저 해바라기처럼.

내가 다른 길 갈까 봐
까맣게 타버린 씨앗들
해바라기는 기도하고 있구나.

Sunflower

Only looking up at the sun
Lives the sunflower.
Could I also live just looking upon you?

Seeing nothing else
Only but the sun
Just like that sunflower.

That I would falter down a different path
With the blackened sunburnt seeds,
The sunflower prays for me.

새벽의 희망

허깨비 새벽너머
꽃잎에 맺힌
이슬방울에서 흔들리는
자연의 종소리.

새 소리와 어우러져
이슬 속에 비치는 하늘빛 따라
새 아침의 해를 살며시 열어 보이네.

헝클어진 머리를 곱게 빗고
눈부신 아침 해를 맞으러 가세.
오늘은 이슬 같은 눈으로
세상이 맑게 보일거야.

The Hope of Dawn

Past the early morning
Hanging upon the floral petals
Rings from shaking dewdrops
Nature's melody of bells.

Harmonizing with bird songs
The sky light reflecting in the dew
A new dawning sun opens up.

Comb tangled hair
And let us greet the morning sun.
Today with eyes like dew
We shall see the world so clear.

달의 모습

별처럼 애써 찾을 필요 없고
해처럼 눈부시지 않게
달은 늘 너그럽고 편안하지.

후덕한 미소 덕에
매일 밤 넉넉한 위안을 비추는 거울을
하늘에 걸고 잠에 든다.

늘 혼자이지만 채웠다, 비웠다를
반복하여 존재를 알리는
그 모습을 내가 배우고 싶은 달.

고독하지만 외롭지 않은 달,
넓고 환한 그런 마음으로
우리 모두 둥글게 살 수 있다면

The Moon's Shape

No need to strain to search for stars
Not painfully bright like the sun
The moon is always generous and comfortable.

Thanks to its smile benevolent
The mirror that each night shines ample comfort
Is hung upon the sky and falls asleep.

Though always alone, it fills and empties
Repeatedly to share it's always there,
The moon, I hope to learn to do the same.

Alone yet not a lonely moon,
With a heart so big and bright,
If only we could live such a rounded life.

어둠과 침묵

어둠과 짙푸른 빙하
깊고 깊은 고독의 방.

그곳에 침묵의 구슬이 살며시
굴러들어 왔을 때

어둠은 차츰 빛을 발하고
세상은 흰 꽃등처럼 밝아지나니.

어둠 속 침묵은 방황하는
내 영혼을 우주의 온기로 품어주네.

Darkness and Silence

Darkness and a deep sea blue glacier
A deep yet deeper solitary room.

Within that place when
The bead of silence rolls forth

The dark gradually hopes for light
The world brightens like a white flower.

The wandering silence in the dark
Holds my soul with the warmth of the universe.

오른손과 왼손

오른손과 왼손은
통소 (洞簫, Flute) 타고 기도하는
끈끈한 또 하나의 나.

하지만 서로의 체온이 같으려면
빨간 피는 손끝에서 끝으로
몸 한 바퀴를 돌아야하지요.

너도 나도 또 하나의 나
서로가 같은 마음을 품으려면
시를 음미하듯 영혼 한 바퀴를
읽고 돌아야 하지요.

Right Hand and Left Hand

Right hand and left hand
Praying with the melodies of a flute
Are both tightly parts of me.

But for their temperatures to be the same
Red blood must travel from one hand's end to the other
Around the body, one full round trip.

You and I, also parts of the one me
To understand each other's heart
Is like understanding poetry for which
The soul must read, travel the full round trip though all the verse.

행복은 바람 같은 것

행복은 살포시 불어와
강하게 부딪치는 바람의 소리.

이 세상 어떤 것도 너를
다 차지할 순 없다는 것을 알지.

숨결을 담은 생명의 바람으로 불어올 때
우린 멀리 날아야 하네.

뜨거운 구슬땀 식혀주는
노래하는 한 줄기 나눔의 행복 바람으로

Happiness is Like the Wind

Happiness is like what flurries by,
The sound of clashing winds.

Nothing in this world
Can ever fill our whole selves up.

When the gust of lively breath does blow
Far away must we all fly.

Cooling down hot beads of sweat
The singing wind that shares happiness.

초봄을 기다리며

살짝 초봄을 넘겨보는
2월의 담장 위에
지난 가을 말라버린 박 넝쿨처럼
남겨진 지난겨울 미련의 흔적.

아쉬움 뒤로 하고 다시 꿈꿔보는 푸르름
희망의 생명 안고 먼 길 달려온 햇빛이
텅 빈 마른 잿빛 화단 밑에
초봄 내음 가득한 온기를 불어 넣어주네.

Waiting for Early Spring

Softly turning into early spring
Over the fence of February
Like the dried up pumpkin vines of fall
The fond traces of fall left behind.

Leaving behind regrets, the greens dreaming once again
The sun that with the hope of life has traveled from afar,
Beneath the emptied dried up flower bed
Into the dirt it fills the energy of early spring.

자존감이 준 선물

자존심이 무겁다는 이유로
자존감을 두고
등산을 떠났습니다.

험한 산행 길에 미끄러진 자존심을
산은 인정해 주지 않아 가슴에
아픈 상처가 남았습니다.

상처투성이로 다시 돌아온
자존심에게 바다 같은 자존감이
푸른 입김으로 상처를 다독입니다.

자존감과 다시 떠난 산행 길엔
꿀 내음 공기, 새들의 오페라를
감상할 수 있었습니다.

상처는 거품 닮은 구름타고
멀리멀리 날아갔습니다.
자존감은 자존심의 어깨를 꼭 감싸주었습니다.

The Gift From Self-Esteem

That Pride was heavy enough,
Self-esteem was left behind
From the trek upon the mountain hike.

Pride that slipped on the treacherous mountain climb,
The mountain did not acknowledge
So the heart was scarred, felt only pain.

Returning back with scars all o'er
To Pride, Self-esteem is like the ocean
That with its blue breath consoles the scars.

With Self-esteem, on that hike again
Honey-like air, the opera of birds
Were able to be enjoyed.

The scars, on foam-like clouds,
Floated far and far away.
As Self-esteem tightly embraced Pride's shoulders.

봄의 소리

초봄 개울에 앉아
살얼음을 바라보며
슬픔이 깊을수록
삶 또한 아름다운 것이라고
흔적 없이 냇물이 되어
사라진 살얼음의
지난겨울 이야기가
아쉬운 듯 물속에 녹아내립니다.
이제는 조금씩 가까워지는
나의 봄 소리가 개울 위에 맴돕니다.

The Sound of Spring

Sitting by the stream of early spring
As I look upon the thin ice caps
The deeper sadness is
The more beautiful life is too
Without a trace, becomes a stream
The melted ice cap gone
A winter story passed
As though with some regret, into water it does melt.
Now that which closer does approach
My sound of spring lingers upon the stream.

아보카도

거친 껍질 속 안에는
연한 녹두 빛 아보카도의
녹아내리는 휴식의 한입.

쓴맛, 단맛, 짠맛으로 잃었던
자연의 맛을 찾아내는 정이 고운 맛.

가라앉은 안개 빛 외로움이 드리울 때
아보카도 벗이 그립습니다.

Avocado

Beneath rough skin
Avocado's soft mung bean flesh
Melts in one effortless mouthful.

Bitter, sweet, salty tastes that were forgotten,
Recalling nature's flavors, the savory affectionate taste.

Like a light submerging fog, when loneliness creeps in
A friendship soft like that of the avocado is missed.

이젠 느낄 수 있어야 하네

밤새 고뇌의 파편을 맞으며 뒤척일 때
번민 없이 잠듦에 감사 할 줄 알며

아픔에 떨며 먹지 못할 때
풍요로운 맛의 소중함을 알며

고갈된 숨결로 헐떡일 때
영혼까지 달게 하는 공기의 참맛을 알며

불타는 사막 속에서 목마름을 격고야
똑똑 물방울 소리마저 꿀맛임을 알아차리지.

헤아릴 수 없이 조용히 쏟아지는 축복을
이젠 느낄 수 있어야 하네.
살아 있는 모든 생명은

Now It Must Be Felt

When restless in agony all night,
One is thankful for the worry-free nights

When shivering in pain, unable to eat,
One values each of the flavorful tastes

When panting out of exhaustion,
One tastes the sweetness of air upon the soul

Only having endured thirst at a blazing desert
Does one realize the sweet sounds of water drops.

The countless blessings that pour forth
One should now be able to notice.
All the living that so lives.

Moonbow, Photograph by Pak Family

Part 3

파랑새
BLUEBIRD

나의 양식

시 한편이 완성될 때마다
내 노트북에 쌓인 내 마음의 양식.
겨울 양식 준비하는
농부의 뿌듯한 마음처럼

서랍 속에 살짝 잠들어 있는
노트북은 깨워 양식을
넣고는 다시 펴 보고 곱씹는
아삭거리는 단맛.

한 편 한 편 쌓여 갈 때마다
든든해지는 나의 영혼
모두들 마음 배고픔에 뒤척이는 밤
난 맛난 양식, 시가 있어 고독하지 않네.

My Food

Each time a poem is complete,
Within my notebook fills up my food.
Like the farmers' own proud hearts
As they stock up their winter food.

Inside the drawer, the napping notebook
Is woken up, to place more food upon its pages
And to open and peruse the words,
Tasting crunchy and so sweet.

Each page by page that gets filled up
My soul gets comforted
All other hungry hearts in restless nights
I with my tasty food, my poems, do not feel loneliness.

파랑새

파랑새 귀는 푸른 숲
푸른 귀 없인 사슴들의 속삭이는
속마음을 알길 없지요.

나의 등은 파랑새 날개
당신을 태워주니
푸른 등 없인 나무 위로
올라갈 수 없지요.

나의 머리는 푸른 나무
당신의 둥지를 틀게 하여
푸른 머리 없인
이 추운 삶속에서
나의 온정을
느낄 수 없겠지요.

Bluebird

A bluebird's ear is a blue-green forest
Without these beryl ears, mutterings and
The inner thoughts of deer cannot be understood.

My back is the bluebird's wings
That which takes you upon some flights,
Without my cobalt back,
Above the treetops I cannot fly.

My head is an evergreen tree
That upon its branches holds your nest
Without this conifer head
In this chilly life,
My warmth
cannot be felt.

바다 진주

쓴 바닷물 마시며
모래알 닮은 하얀 침묵 지키며
찬 바다노래 삼켰던 바다 진주.

바다 속 가장 고운 조개 빛으로
보석의 단단함을 빚어낸
마음에 행복 열매가 되었지요.

가슴 안에 인고의 달품은 바다 진주는
아픔을 모르고 진주 없던 조개가 꿈꾸던
화안한 빛 가진 조개 열매를 만났지요.

Ocean Pearl

Drinking the bitter seawater
Protecting white sand-like silence
The pearl that's swallowed the cold sea song.

With the loveliest shell color of the sea
Produced the hardness of gemstones
It became the heart's fruit of happiness.

The pearl that endured all within the heart
Not knowing pain without the pearl, the shell
Met its brilliant fruit that it had always dreamt of.

할머니의 손

실타래 돌리는 할머니 손
이마의 주름타고
사랑으로 연결된 마음의 고향.

할머니 손에 흔들리던 흰 묵주
여윈 목줄타고 들려오는
채송화 씨같이 작고 많은 바램들.

잠결에 전해오는 할머니 손 온기에
꿈길 따라 펼쳐내는 절절한
자식걱정, 자식사랑.

Grandma's Hand

Grandma's hand that turns the threads
Riding wrinkles upon her forehead
The heart's hometown that with love was braided.

The white rosary that loosely hung from my grandma's hand
Down the thin thread
Many like the rose moss' seed, were all the prayers heard.

Coming like breezes, the heat of my grandma's hand
Following the unfolding dreams, endearing
Care for her children, love for her children.

나의 것으로

욕심을 살살 마음에서 밀어내니
하늘의 해, 달, 별과
땅 위의 바위, 나무, 꽃들이
모두 나를 풀색으로 물들였네.

집착에서 훌훌 떠나고 보니
바다의 파도, 모래, 바람과
삶의 기쁨, 행복, 사랑이
온통 나의 것으로 살포시 찾아드네.

버리고나니 채워짐으로 넘쳐 남을
나는 깨달았네.

To Make Mine

As I pushed greed away from my heart
The sky's sun, moon, stars and
Above land, the rocks, trees, flowers
Have all painted me in green.

As I have left far from obsession,
The ocean's waves, sand, wind and
Life's joy, happiness, love
Have all quietly come to be mine.

Having thrown it all aside, Of the overflowing fullness
I did realize.

별똥별 쏟아지는 산

그리움의 덫에 갇혀 있다면
가장 깨끗한 눈으로
별똥별 쏟아지는 산위로 가보세요.

희망의 꿈을 갖고 있다면
가장 맑은 눈으로
별똥별 쏟아지는 산위로 가보세요.

칠흑 하늘에 빨간 금이 가기
빛줄기 품은 고요한 하늘에
경이로운 출렁임 이 생겨납니다.

그리움 품은 이에겐 반짝이는 위로를
희망에 찬 이에겐 빛나는 포옹을
찰나에 왔다 가는 하늘의 사랑, 별똥별.

The Shooting Star Mountain

If trapped by grief,
With the cleanest eyes,
Go up the mountain showering with shooting stars.

If with a hopeful dream,
With the clearest eyes
Go up the mountain showering with shooting stars.

Upon the pitch black sky, a red scar goes
The silent night that holds star lights
A phenomenal burst of light will come.

For those that harbor grief, the sparkling comfort
For those filled with hope, the bright embrace
That instantaneously comes and goes is the sky's love, shooting stars.

햇볕만 느끼세요

해님의 황홀함을 직접 바라보면
눈의 영혼이 빠져나가
다시는 해님을 볼 수 없음을
해님이 비추어낸
정겨운 햇발의 온기만 느끼세요.
그것이면 충분합니다.

붙어 다니는 한 쌍의 노루도
너무 가깝게 쳐다보면
도리어 차디찬 화를 부름을
그저 서로 보내는
따는 정만 달게 나누세요.
그것이면 충분합니다.

Feel Only the Sun

If you look directly upon the sun's ecstasy
It forever leaves the eyes
And never again can you see the sun
Just feel the warm sunshine
Of the sun's illumination.
That alone is enough.

Even the pair of deer together as they are,
If at each other, they stare too close
Cold anger is all they may bring
So to each other just
Share affection that is sweet.
That alone is enough.

명상의 숲

명상은 고요한 숲속
크고 작은 나무들의 희로애락이
얼기설기 흔들리고 있다.

흐릿하게 흘러가는 추억과
여린 바람타고 다가오는 미래에
하얗게 텅 비어진 마음의 숲.

아름드리나무에 기대어 듣는
봄꿈 같은 현재의 나지막한
휘파람 소리.

Meditative Forest

Meditation, a quiet forest
Emotions of trees large and small
Sway this way, that way there.

Memories floating dimly away
Future approaching upon delicate winds
Emptied white, my heart's forest.

Leaning upon an olden tree
Hearing what's like the dreams of spring
Today's soft whistling sounds.

일장춘몽이었다고

꿈틀대는 캔년의 핏줄기
꼭 그림 같다는 착각을 하지요.
생명이 묻어나는 명화는
꼭 튀어 나올 것 같은 현실 같지요.

종소리 빗기던 초원의 꿈속은
현실인 듯 하구요.
푸근한 현실에선
꼭 꿈만 같다 하지요.

꿈과 현실이 뒤엉킨 뒤안길에
한낱 일장춘몽이었다고 읊조리시던
백발노인의 뒷모습이 어릿어릿
맴도는 꿈같은 봄날입니다.

I Have an Empty Fantasy

The meandering canyon veins
Is always mistaken as a painting.
The artwork that life paints
Always seems to come to life.

That by bell sounds was combed, the meadow's dream
Seems to become reality.
Within the comforting reality,
It always feels just like a dream.

In the backstreets where dream and reality have tangled
A gray-haired man so chants 'twas just an empty dream
As his appearance from behind dimly
Meanders on a dream-like day of spring.

향기 품은 이슬로

새벽녘 빨간 장미에 맺힌 이슬을
유리병에 모아 담으면
아마 발그스레한 장미향이 나겠지요?

초록 새순에 수줍게 맺힌 이슬을
유리병에 모아 담으면
아마 파릇한 풀 내음이 피어오르겠지요?

맑은 눈에 맺히는 기쁨의 이슬로
새로이 태어나 촉촉이 세상 적시는
향기품은 이슬로 살고 싶습니다.

The Dew that Bore Fragrance

Near dawn, dew that upon a red rose formed
If gathered into a glass jar
Would it not smell of the crimson rose?

For the dew formed upon a shy green bud
If gathered into a glass jar
Would it not have the aroma of fresh greenery?

For dew formed from happiness upon clear eyes
Like newly born moisture that infuses the world,
I wish to live as the fragrant dew.

구름처럼

구름처럼 자기 마음속을 잘
표현하는 화가가 있을까요?

연파랑 하늘 아래 화실을 갖고
시시각각 고운 색으로 펼쳐내는 마법의 손.

일초도 쉼 없이 변화시키는 작품 덕에
화실 찾는 새들은 무료하지 않지요.

볼 살 통통한 꼬마에겐 동물인형을,
부끄럼 많은 소녀에겐 꽃다발을.

구름처럼 넘쳐나는 재주로
움직이는 시 한번 써 보았으면…

Like the Cloud

Is there an artist that like a cloud
Expresses its inner thoughts so well?

With a studio under the sky blue sky
Each moment does the magic hand lay lovely hues

Thanks to the ever changing art
Birds that at the studio do rest don't tire.

For the plump cheek child with the stuffed animal,
Who is so shy, a bunch of flowers.

Like the cloud, with overflowing talent
If only I could write such a moving poem...

아침을 맞이하며

아침이 오면 두 손은 하늘의 꽃
뭉게구름을 가슴에 한 아름 안고
노래하는 개울에 두 발 담고
온몸으로 삶을 느껴보자.

또 하나의 오늘을 얻기 위해
스치는 바람에게 인사 건네고
햇빛에 취하고
나무들과 따뜻한 포옹을.

뛰는 희망 속에 하루를 열면
모든 것을 얻는 것과 같다.

As I Welcome the Morning

When mornings come, two hands like flowers in the sky
Hug to one's heart an armful of fluffy clouds
Within a singing stream, dipping both feet
Let us feel life with all our selves.

In order to receive another day that is today
Greet the passing wind
Get drunk with the sunny light
And embrace the trees with warmth.

Opening a day with running hope,
Is the same as having everything.

밤을 맞이하며

밤이 되면 두 눈 속엔 달님 담고
두 귀는 별들의 속삭임에 젖어들고
하늘을 음미하며
온몸으로 삶을 느껴보자.

또 하나의 오늘을 완성하기 위해
그윽한 밤 향기에 목욕하고
고요와 어깨동무하며
나하고 정겨운 대화를.

감사하는 평화 속에 하루를 닫으면
새로운 내일이 방긋이 웃고 있지.

As I Welcome the Night

When it becomes night, I place the moon within my eyes
Two ears listen to murmurs of the stars
As I appreciate the sky
Let us feel life with all our selves.

In order to finish another of today
Bathe in the fragrance of the graceful night
Embrace the shoulders of the Calm
As we exchange some fond remarks.

When I close a day with thankful peace,
The upcoming day smiles happily.

추억은

차갑던 비가 땅에겐 따뜻한 사랑이었다는 것을,
따갑던 햇살이 녹엽에겐 귀한 식량이었다는 것을,
시끄럽던 새들의 노래가 들녘의 아늑한 위안이었다는 것을.

그들이 모두 함께 사라져 버리니
평범한 웃음소리가 달았다는 것을 있을 땐 몰랐네.
추억은 그대 머릿속에 찾아와 뿌리를 내리네.

Memories

That the frigid rain was warm love to the ground,
That the burning sun was precious food to green foliage,
That the noisy bird songs were comfort to the fields.

Until all of you had gone away
It was not known how sweet the casual laughters were.
Only in your minds can memories enroot.

눈이 오면

눈이 옵니다.
내 마음에 흰 기쁨의 불을 지르며.

태양의 꿈과 바람의 소원이 하늘에서 만나
하얀 희망으로 태어나 나부낍니다.

눈이 찾아오지 않았다면
추운 비에 젖어 무거워졌을 나의 옷.

움츠리는 겨울 날 훌훌 벗어 던진
묵직한 멍에의 옷.

눈이 옵니다.
내 마음에 녹아내리는 하얀 희망 전해주려고.

When it Snows

Snow is coming down.
As it kindles my heart's happy fire.

Upon the sky, the sun's dream and wind's wish
Meet and give rise to hope.

Had the snow not come
The cold rain would have heavily drenched my clothes.

On a shivering winter day
Clothes thrown off and tossed aside.

Snow is coming down.
To deliver melting pure hope to my heart.

선인장 열매

태양의 피를 머금은
사막의 빨간 보석, 선인장 열매.

열기에 지친 생명을
먹여 살려 내고자.

단단한 침묵의 결심으로
끌어 올린 가시 속 생명수.

가시관 쓰고 푸른 종소리 고결히
지켜낸 붉은 모습이 꼭 그분을 닮았구나.

The Cactus Fruit

The blood of Sun, consumed and captured
Within the desert's little red gem.

That which exists to feed and give
To lives exhausted from the heat.

Without a word, the little one doth harvest water
From the very depths, hugging it close, precious,
within its body.

Upon its head a crown of thorns, its red cactus fruits
That it's kept, the crimson selves look just like Him.

Snowy Forest, Photograph by Pak Family

Part 4

그 손, 그 발
THAT HAND, THAT FOOT

그 손, 그 발

손이 참 고맙지만
발 또한 고맙지.

손은 가까이서 사랑받지만
발은 늘 뒷전이지.

손은 표정 많은 어머니라면
발은 무표정한 아버지.

생각해보니 채워지는 고마움
무거운 육신을 불평 없이
매일 뚜벅 뚜벅 같이 가 주는 감사함이.

나 또한 잊혀진 발처럼
누군가의 버팀목이 될 수 있을까?

That Hand, That Foot

Though thankful for my hand
I'm also grateful for my foot.

Though the hand close by receives much love
The foot is always last.

If the hand, an expressive mother
The foot, a blank-faced father.

Upon thinking, the gratefulness that fills
For without complaints, it carries the heavy body
Lumbering with gratitude everyday.

Could I too, like the forgotten foot,
Be that support for someone else?

마른 꽃으로

종일 바삐 뛰다가
바람 소리에 잠시 멈췄네.

바람의 질투로 견딤을 내려놓고
바람길 타고 데구루루 굴러온 꽃송이.

곧 시들었을 꽃송이는 바람 덕에
고운 색깔 품은 마른 꽃으로 다시 태어났네.

적적한 정원 한 구석에서
웃음 많은 소녀의 나무 책상 위로.

참다움이란 견디어내는 인내라고
또 다른 매력의 마른 꽃이란 이름으로.

With the Dried Flower

Busily running about all day
But at the sound of wind, for a moment paused.

With the help of wind, set aside jealousy
The flower bud, tossed by the wind rolled in

The bud that would have withered soon,
Was reborn a new dried flower thanks to the wind.

In the corner of a lonely garden,
Upon the wooden desk of a bubbly girl lands the flower.

Truthfulness that has endured patience
Is another charm of the dried flower.

감사와 미안이란 말

살구 씨처럼 마음에 지닌 생각들
왠지 꺼내기 어색해합니다.

나도 또 그대도 듣고 싶고
느끼고 싶은 상대의 마음 소리.

꼭꼭 숨어 있다 용기 내어 나온
깃털처럼 가슴 따뜻해지는.

마음속 서랍 속 말
감사합니다! 미안합니다!

Thank You and Sorry

Carrying in the heart like an apricot seed
That to take out is a bit awkward.

I want to hear you once again
And feel the sound of your heart.

Bravely sharing what was hidden deep within
Like down feathers, makes the heart warm.

One's most inner thoughts, words tucked in drawers
Thank you! I'm Sorry!

가을밤에

가을밤이면 츠르르릇 다가오는
벌레들의 이야기 소리
마음 담아 듣다보니
수려한 서정시 한편이 쓰여지지.

고요를 업고 번져나는
가락 타는 노래 속에
세월 가는 소리, 세월 오는 소리가 들리네.

허공에 남는 푸른 여운 속에
가을밤이 감칠 맛 나는
세월 익는 소리로 영글어 가네.

On an Autumn Night

On an autumn night,
Storytellings of the bugs
Upon listening to them
A glorious epic poem comes out.

With silence, that spreads out
That rides the melody
Sounds of what has passed, sounds of what will come is heard.

The blue imagery that silence leaves behind
The hidden taste that autumn leaves
The sound of ripening time goes.

은행잎을 보며

찾아오자마자
잡고 싶었던 열망
너무 벅차서 포기해 버린 꿈
청록 물감 풀어 넣은
호수에서 다시 찾아 헤매네.

물둘레 물결마다 들어 있는
무지개들이 흔들리며
들려주는 노랑 은행잎의
물결 웃음소리.

묵묵히 열매 맺어 그 몫을 다하고
초록 잎에서 인고의 시간 먹고
노랑 잎으로 변신해 보여주는
여유 있는 물위의 춤사위를 배우고 싶네.

Looking Upon the Gingko Leaf

As soon as it comes
The longing to hold on
The dream too great that was given up
In the lake where turquoise watercolor
Was released, I search again.

Within each ripple
The rainbow that shimmers
The yellow gingko leaf
Listens to the giggling waters.

Diligently made a fruit,
The green leaves that ingested enduring times
Shows their yellowed selves,
Lightheartedly dancing above waters, that I so wish to learn.

잡초

한 치 뒤로 물러서면
성큼 오르는 잡초들
가늠키 어려운 솟구치는 잡초더미.

한시라도 마음 안 쓰면
잡초로 덮어지는
나의 애틋한 화단.

내 마음 정원 속에 스며나는
빛깔과 향 내음을 그대로 지키려면
상동상동 뽀족이 오른 잡념을
바지런히 잘라내야 하네.

Weeds

Taking a step back one sees
The weeds that have grown so tall
Endured all difficulties, the pile of weeds.

Not a moment to relax
The weeds that took over
My fond little garden lot.

Within the garden of my heart
In order to maintain shine and fragrance too
The sharp worries and distractions
Must be cut right away.

산들바람

무료한 오후 문득
바람이 스치며 선물한
나무의 풋풋한 기품의 향기에 잠시
숨을 고르고 나를 바라봅니다.

여유로이 손짓하는 야자수 잎처럼
큰마음으로 세상을 보았는지?
혹 가시 많은 선인장처럼
따갑지는 않았는지?

존재를 최소로 알리는
산들바람같이 누군가에게
살며시 용기의 향기로
젖게 하는 미풍이 되길.

Breeze

Upon a free afternoon, suddenly
A breeze goes by
A tree that by the graceful scent
For a moment catches its breath and looks at me.

Like the palm leaf that freely gestures forth
Had I seen the world with as big a heart?
Perhaps like the thorny cactus
Was I not prickly too?

Like the breeze that through vegetation
Reveals its very existence,
I hope that I too can for someone else
Be a zephyr that carries encouraging aroma through.

어제, 오늘, 내일

지내다 보면 까마귀처럼
까맣게 잊혀진 어제의 모습
제대로 만나지도 못하고
작은 일에 넋을 팔아 허망하게 보냈네.

오늘의 하루는 지난날의
하루하루를 딛고 생겨난 귀한 날
감사한 그대, 오늘과 손잡고
하찮은 바람에 흔들림 없이 보내리.

오늘과 빛을 나누다 보니
찬란한 내일의 태양이 노랑 빛줄기를
바다위에 갈래갈래 뿌려 놓고
금빛 날개 춤추며 오르네.

내일은 금빛 학처럼
광채 내는 모습으로 마지할거야.

Now, Today, Tomorrow

Once passed, like the crow
Is as dark, yesterday's appearance
Unable to fully meet
The small happenings that in vain did pass.

Today is a day that's passed the yesterday
Passing day by day, born a precious new day
Holding hands with gratefulness,
That without a wind of worry to shake today shall pass.

Having shared light with today
A shining tomorrow's yellow sunbeam
Sprays on the ocean waves,
Upon which the gold wings dance.

Tomorrow like a golden crane
I shall face it with a glowing self.

사랑의 힘

바다의 숨결은 대지의 바람과
청량한 호흡 덕에
땅은 생명을 낳아냅니다.

은빛 달빛이 파도를 끌어올림에
그 끌림으로 등 푸른 거북이는
생명을 낳으려고 모래로 오릅니다.

서로 주고받는 우주사랑의 힘 덕에
오늘도 숨을 머금은 생명들은
새로운 날을 가슴 떨며 여는가 봅니다.

The Strength of Love

The ocean's breath with the earth's wind
By virtue of the cool clear breath,
The land gives birth to life.

The silver moonlight that pulls up waves
The blue-back sea turtle rides that force
To sands to give birth to life.

By the universe's love that is exchanged
All the lives that contain the breath
Look upon a new day with fluttering hearts.

어둠속에도

모두들 밝음만 찾아가고
어둠은 소외될 때가 종종 있죠.
눈을 맑게 씻고 눅눅한 어둠을 보니
솜털같이 다정할 때도 있답니다.

밝아서 들리지 않았던 귓전 속삭임들
어둠속 별빛들이 얼마나
정겹게 말을 건네는지 모릅니다.

어둠을 곱씹을 때 비로소
느낄 수 있는 넉넉한 감사의 향기,
새 둥지같이 포근하고 따스한
귀엣말 소리를.

Even in the Dark

As all seek only light
The dark is often left behind.
Seeing the damp dark with clear washed eyes
It can be friendly like cotton soft.

So bright that whispers were not heard
The star lights in the dark
How tenderly they do speak.

Only when one dwells upon the dark
The grateful scent that can be felt
Cozy and warm like a bird's nest
The sound of whisperings.

우리 가족

따스한 주황 불빛이 흘러나오는
촛불 같은 우리 가족,
입안에서 살며시 녹는 영혼의
사탕 같은 우리 가족이란 말.

티격태격 거리며 튀어 떨어진
작은 불똥들이 차곡차곡히 쌓여
어느덧 시린 등을 녹이는
온기 가득한 아궁이가 되었네.

각자 다른 눈으로 모두 한곳을
바라보는 우리 가족
오늘도 촛농 흐르는 소리와 초 타는
내음이 가슴 녹이며 정겹게 들리네.

Our Family

Like the warm amber rays flowing
From a candle light is our family
The word "family", melting upon my mouth
Like the sweet candy of the soul.

The bantering sparks that leapt
From the flame and piled up
Had become a warming furnace
That warmed our chilly backs.

Each with our own eyes, our family looks at the same place
Again today, the dripping sound of guttered wax
With the burning smell of candle stick,
Does melt our hearts and sound cozy.

사랑의 딸들

한겹 한겹 쌓여
애절함으로 피어난 꽃들.

보내도 보내도
끝이 없는 나의 마음.

맑은 공기 마시고 자라 이슬 같은
영혼으로 거듭 태어난 딸들.

복된 말씀 거름 삼아
찰 지게 영근 푸르른 마음.
영롱한 하늘 바라보며 물든 두 눈을
들여다보니 투명한 하늘 창이 들어 있네.

한 올 한 올 땋아 지은
나의 절절한 사랑의 딸들.

Daughters of Love

Petal by petal,
Flowers bloomed through endearment.

Though sent away,
My heart's love that reaches out does never cease.

Breathing in fresh air, grown up like dew
My daughters born with whole new souls.

Fertilizing holy words, soaked in to grow
Resilient, ripened, azure awe-inspiring hearts
Their pigmented eyes that look at the iridescent sky
Upon looking into them, the sky's unstained glass was found.

Stitched one by one were built
My beloved girls of love

나의 빛, 나의 친구

멀리 떨어져 있어도 달은 늘
가까이에서 나에게 위안이 듯
나의 친구 또한 나의 빛이지.

힘들 땐 낭랑한 목소리에
푸른 잔디같이
펼쳐내는 바른 마음.

기쁜 일엔 서슴없이
짙은 마음 담아
박수 보내주는 바다 같은 친구.

나 또한 친구가 지쳐 왔을 때
몽글몽글 오르는 옹달샘으로
친구의 목을 축일 수 있는 단물이고 싶다.

서로의 항해에 따뜻한 손을
내밀어 줄 수 있는 서로의
희망의 시 같은 존재로.

My Light, My Friend

Though far away, the moon
As though close by, provides comfort
And is both my friend and light.

When times are hard, its clear voice
Like an expansive, emerald grassy field
Spreads out its righteous heart.

In joyful times, with no hesitation
A full genuine heart, wide like the ocean
Sends out its great applause.

When my friend tires and comes to me
I, bubbling up like a spring,
Hope to be sweet water that moistens my friend's throat.

In this naval journey, our lending hands
That reach out to one another,
Like the existence of hope within poetry.

싹

용서의 싹이 돋아난다면
살포시 물을 주세요.

싹이 시들면 희망의 꽃을 볼 수 없듯이
그 후엔 향기 잃은 화초일 뿐이니까요.

두려움의 싹이 움튼다면
살며시 싹을 뽑으세요.

덩굴이 무성해지면 그 속에 갇히게 되어
해가 사라진 하늘만 남을 뿐이기에.

화해의 싹을 보기 위해
솔솔 씨를 뿌려 보세요.

표용의 싹이 없는 삶은
달이 사라진 어두운 밤하늘과 같기에.

Sprout

If a sprout of forgiveness buds
Gently give it water.

For if withers the sprout, so also goes the flower of hope
And it becomes just a plant that's lost its fragrance.

If in fear the sprouts do bud
Pull the plant with stealth.

For as the vines grow thick, trapped they get
And a sunless sky is all that shall remain.

To see a sprout of reconciliation
Softly spread seeds about.

For a life without a sprout of generosity
Is the same as a night sky without the moon.

빗속의 나의 방

빗속에서의 젖은 세상의 느낌
오롯이 우산 속에 나만의 방이 생긴다.
세상과 나의 방은 빗물 물안개로 인해
서로의 공간이 둘로 나뉘고

밝은 날 느끼지 못했던
아늑하고 촉촉한 나만의
안개 같은 비밀 우산 속 방에선
때론 우리는 모두 행복한 혼자라는 것을.

My Room Within the Rain

Within the rain, the feeling of a dampened world
Only under the umbrella does my room form.
The world and my room with rain and fog
Dividing up each other's space

Not having felt a brightened day
My own cozy and moist room
Under the umbrella, secretive like fog
We can feel that we are happy single individuals.

선한 눈망울

장엄한 자연 속에선
우리들의 눈은
선한 눈망울로 바뀌지.

도시와 엘리베이터 속에서
느끼지 못했던
순수한 눈망울들.

나뭇잎 사이로 보이는
먹구름 뒤쪽에서
은빛으로 빛을 내는
숲의 슬기를.

맑은 눈망울로 받아들이니
이웃들의 뽀얀 미소가
기쁨을 쏟아내는
보석함이 되었네.

우리 모두는 자연 안에선
선한 눈망울을 가졌네.

Good-natured Eye

Within grand nature
Our eyes
Become good-natured eyes.

Within the city and elevator
The pure eyes
That could not be felt.

Seen between the leaves
From the farther corners of shadows
Shining silver lights
Wisdom of the forest.

Receiving with clear eyes
My neighbor's milky smiles
That pour out happiness
Have become a jewel box.

All of us in nature
Have got good-natured eyes.

■ 서평

박은희의 시세계

조 윤 호
(시인. 해외문학 발행인)

　박은희 시인의 시세계는 한마디로 큰 공감을 준다. 그의 시를 읽어보면, "나를 낮추면 세상이 나를 높여주고, 나를 높여주면 세상이 나를 낮춘다."는 인생의 깨달음을 담고 있기 때문이다.
　그의 대표적인 시에 속하는 「파랑새」는 희망과 행복이라는 상징적인 의미가 있다. 파랑새의 귀가 푸른 숲이 되어야 사슴들의 속삭이는 속마음을 알 수 있다. 나의 등도 파랑새 날개가 되어야 당신을 태워주어 나무 위로 올라갈 수 있다. 나의 머리는 푸른 나무가 되어야 당신의 둥지를 틀 수가 있다는 것이다. 이처럼 우리가 사는 목적이 바로 행복이므로 내가 남을 위해서 도와야 내가 행복을 누릴 수 있단다. 이것이 바로 박은희 시인의 깊은 인생 통찰의 매력이라 할 수 있다.
　박 시인은 각박한 현실생활에 매달리다 보니 삶의 여유가 없으니 여유 있는 시간을 가져야 행복하단다. 그것이 「새의 노래」이다.

　　　햇볕 욕심에 서로 잎사귀를 넓히던 활엽수

맥없이 가을바람에 퇴색하여 톡톡 떨어지는데

바늘 같은 몸을 줄여 서로 햇볕 양보하던
솔 잎사귀들은 매서운 겨울에도 푸르디푸르네.

겸손함이 솔 향으로 뿜어지니
치유의 초록향이 숲에 가득하네.
「겸손한 솔 잎사귀」 1부

시인은 시 「겸손한 솔 잎사귀」에서도 "햇볕 욕심에 서로 잎사귀를 넓히던 활엽수는 가을이 되면 퇴색하여 바람에 톡톡 떨어진다. 이와는 달리 햇볕을 양보하던 솔 잎사귀는 매서운 겨울에도 푸르디 푸르다"는 것을 보여주고 있다. 더구나 겸손함이 솔 향으로 뿜어지니 치유의 초록향이 숲에 가득하다고 우리에게 타이른다.

박 시인은 부부 문제에도 관심을 보여준다. 그의 시 「부부」에서 보면, "추위와 무더위 속에서 서로의 온기와 그늘이 되어 쓸어주고, 치워 주며 곰삭아 가는 다정한 하나같은 둘"이 될 때 부부는 행복하다는 것이다.

또 세상에는 남에게 상처를 주는 말을 함부로 한다. 하지만, 상처를 받은 사람은 결코 행복할 수가 없음을 박은희 시인은 일깨워 준다. 그의 시 「바위처럼」에서 "소리 없이 마음으로 말하는 바위처럼 인생의 그 자리를 침묵으로 지키고 싶습니다."라고 희망한다. 그의 시 「침묵」을 음미하면, "이 세상에 진리로 말하는 것보다 더 큰 기쁨은 없다"면서 "당신과 나누는 말보다 더 큰 기쁨은 나도 찾지 못했지만, 허공을 떠도는 사랑이란 말도 마음에 상처를 입히고, 격려를 내세운 말도 침묵하는 것보다 더 아플 때도 있으니 말조심과 입조심을 하란다.

행복한 인생을 살아가려면 무엇보다 내가 변해야 된다는 것이다. 시 「내가 변하니」에서 시인은 "내가 먼저 변하니 세상

의 모진 말들이 수정 은빛 종소리 되고, 그 맑은 종소리는 희
망의 메아리가 되어 돌아온단다.

> 채송화 앞에 서면
> 고개 숙여 보게 된다.
>
> 초록빛 나무의 푸른 그림자 사이로
> 낮아지는 내 모습.
>
> 가끔 겸손하여
> 낮추는 이들 중에
>
> 나도 함께 서서
> 채송화를 바라보네.
>
> 「채송화 닮은 사람」

박 시인은 시 「채송화 닮은 사람」에서 행복의 조건을 제시하고 있다. "채송화 앞에 서면 고개 숙여 보게 되는 것은 초록빛 나무의 푸른 그림자 사이로 낮아지는 내 모습을 떠올린다. 가장 겸손하여 낮추는 이들 중에 나도 함께 서서 채송화를 바라보고 있다. 행복이란 오직 큰 것만이 아니라 작은 것에도 행복이 있다고 역설한다. 박 시인의 시 「꽃송이의 가르침」을 읽으면, "작은 꽃들도 꽃이 피고, 그 작은 꽃도 꽃잎마다 작은 향을 풍긴다"면서 "꽃이 작아도 우리에게 아름다움만 주고 가네"라고 노래한다. 큰 꽃만 꽃이 아니라 작은 꽃도 꽃이니 너무 욕심내지 말라는 시적 의미가 읽혀진다.

> 손이 참 고맙지만
> 발 또한 고맙지.
>
> 손은 가까이서 사랑받지만
> 발은 늘 뒷전이지.

손은 표정 많은 어머니라면
발은 무표정한 아버지.

생각해보니 채워지는 고마움
무거운 육신을 불평 없이
매일 뚜벅 뚜벅 같이 가 주는 감사함이.

나 또한 잊혀진 발처럼
누군가의 버팀목이 될 수 있을까?

「그 손, 그 발」

　박은희 시인의 「그 손, 그 발」에서 손은 어머니와 발은 아버지를 은유적으로 표현한 아름다운 시다. "무거운 육신을 불평 없이 매일 뚜벅뚜벅 같이 가 주는 감사함을 본받아 무표정한 아버지처럼 나도 잊혀진 발이 되어 누군가의 버팀목이 되고 싶단다.

혼자서도 지나는 이에게
늘 평온한 미소
나누어 주는 선한 들꽃.

언제 꺾어질 줄 모르는
변화에도 당당함으로
의연히 감사로 피어있네.

「들꽃처럼」 1부

　시인의 시 「들꽃처럼」은 아무 욕심 부리지 않고 오히려 베풀고 사는 삶이 행복하다는 인생의 시적 주제를 형상화한 감동적인 시다.
　박은희 시인의 시는 감성적인 시를 통해 우리에게 체험하게 한다. 그 표현력 또한 적절한 이미지로 하여금 행복의 조건을

깊이 터치하게 하고 있다. 이처럼 생동감 있게 시적 형상화를 보여 줌으로써 우리를 깊은 사색과 감동으로 매료시킨다.

  박은희 시인의 시적 특징은 무엇보다 간결함에 있다. 대부분의 시가 4연과 5연으로 함축되어 있어 지루함을 느끼지 않는다.

  진실한 행복을 추구한다면 스스로 낮아지고, 먼저 나누어 주며, 욕심도 버리란다. 그리고 상처 주는 말 대신 침묵하며, 인생이 무엇보다 깨달아보라고 노래한 시들이라 감동이 크다.

◪ Book Review

Eun Hee Pak's Poetic World

Yoon-Ho Cho
(Poet. Korean Expatriate Literary Publisher)

　Put simply, Poet Eun Hee Pak's poetry reveals great compassion. Her poems remind readers of the saying that "If I lower myself, the world raises me up. If I raise myself, the world lowers me down," which reveals her enlightened view on life. "Bluebird," one of her more prominent poems, symbolizes hope and happiness. She says the bluebird's ear must become the green forest in order to hear and understand the inner thoughts and feelings of the deer. She continues and says her back must be the bluebird's wings in order to fly you atop the trees. Her head must become the green treetops so that she can hold your nest. As such, she expresses that given the goal of life is to achieve happiness, helping others is a way to reach that goal. This is precisely Poet Eun Hee Pak's deep insight on life that is so charismatic.

Poet Pak believes that amidst surviving a difficult reality, leisure is a rarity. Consequently, she shares that one must seek leisure in order to be happy. Such is expressed in her "Bird's Song."

> Greedy for sunlight, the deciduous leaves spread wide open
> So easily do they fall at an autumn breeze
>
> But the thin pine needles that conserve to share sunlight
> Are ever so green amidst winter so fierce
>
> Modesty sprayed through the pine scent
> Fills the forest with a healing green fragrance
> — "Modest Pine Needles," Part 1

In the poem "Modest Pine Needles," the poet writes, "Greedy for sunlight, the deciduous leaves spread wide open, So easily do they fall at an autumn breeze." On the other hand, she shows that the pine needles that share the sunlight "are ever so green amidst winter so fierce." Furthermore, she tells us that modesty in the form of pine fragrance fills the green forest.

Poet Pak also sheds light on her thoughts on the theme of marriage. In her poem "Married Couple," she says, "In the hot and cold / They become each other's shade and heat / Sweeping and cleaning, / Being worn down fondly, two that are like one," to show that being in such a state is a sign that the couple is happy.

Additionally, she states we live in a world in which it's very easy to say hurtful words. But Poet Pak reminds us that the person who is scarred by those words can never be happy. She expresses her hope to be "Like a Boulder", "Without a sound, only speaking with its heart. / Like a boulder, / I wish to silently fulfill the responsibility of life." In her poem "Silence," she writes that "In this world / It is said there is no happiness / Greater than truthful speaking", as "A happiness greater / Than speaking with you / I have not found. / Thrown in the air / Empty words of love / Can dress wounds upon the heart," to express that one must be sincere and careful about what one says.

Another perspective on life she maintained was that she must, at times, adjust her perspective in order to live happily. In "As I Change," the poet explains that "As I change myself / The world's harsh words / Become crystal silver bell sounds / And the clear bell sounds / Become echoes of hope."

> When standing in front of a purslane
> One's head bows down.
>
> Into the green shadows of the trees
> Hides my lowered body.
>
> Among those who at times
> Lower themselves in humility,
>
> I stand with them
> And look upon the purslanes.

—"A Person Like Purslane"

In "A Person Like Purslane," Poet Pak shares her recipe for happiness. She visualizes in "A Person Like Purslane," "When standing in front of a purslane / One's head bows down. / Into the green shadows of the trees / Hides my lowered body." This person stands among those who lower themselves in humility and looks upon the purslane flowers together. She highlights that happiness isn't solely found in the grandiose but also in the small. Her poem "The Teachings of a Blossom" paints, "A small flower
So beautifully has blossomed too. / Even such a tiny flower / Per petal that it has / Gives off a small aroma. / Though little is the blossom, / To us does it give / Beauty and only that." It is not just the big flowers but also the small ones that are flowers. In other words, the writer shares that one shouldn't be too greedy.

    Thought thankful for my hand
    I'm also grateful for my foot

    Though the hand close by receives much love
    The foot is always last

    If the hand, an expressive mother
    The foot, a blank-faced father

    Upon thinking, the gratefulness that fills
    For without complaints, it carries the heavy body
    Lumbering with gratitude everyday

> Could I too, like the forgotten foot,
> Be that support for someone else?
> 　　　　　　　　　　— "That Hand, That Foot"

　　Poet Eun Hee Pak's poem "That Hand, That Foot", in which she metaphorically represents the hand as a mother and foot as a father, is a beautiful work. She writes, "For without complaints, it carries the heavy body / Lumbering with gratitude everyday," to describe the expressionless father who's like the forgotten foot that she wishes to be so she too can be someone's support.

> To those who walk alone
> Always peaceful, joyful music
> The kind wildflower shares
>
> Not knowing when it may be broken
> Confident in the face of change
> Bloomed it has, out of thanksgiving
> 　　　　　　　—"Like the Wildflower," Part 1

　　The poet's work "Like the Wildflower," an awe-inspiring poem themed on life, conveys that living a life of mercy and giving, rather than greed, is a happy life.

　　Poet Eun Hee Pak's poems through her sensible language enable us to truly experience them. Her expressiveness through appropriate images, even on more abstract themes such as the recipes for happiness, allow the reader to more deeply understand her thoughts. Such lively poetic imagery pulls the readers deep into contemplation and causes them to be moved by her messages. Above all, Poet Eun Hee Pak distinguishes herself with her concision. As her poems are generally encapsulated within 4 to 5 stanzas, there is no room for the reader to grow bored.

To seek true happiness, she shares that one must be humble, be the first to share, and leave greed behind. And instead of saying hurtful words, one should remain silent. Most importantly, these poems are greatly awe-inspiring, because they sing about life.

작가에 관하여

박은희 시인은 1961년 서울에서 출생한 여류 시인이다.
박 시인은 George Mason University를 졸업했다.
『해외문학』 신인문학상에 시가 당선 되어 미국 문단에 데뷔했으며 『창조문학』(한국)에서 시부문 신인상을 수상했다.
「해외문인협회」(미국) 회원이다.
시집 「파랑새」 출간.

ABOUT THE AUTHOR

Eun Hee Pak is a poet born in Seoul, South Korea in 1961. She received her Bachelor's degree from George Mason University. In 2017, she won the Korean Expatriate Literary prize and debuted her first poems.

In 2018, she won Creative Literature's "New Poet Award". She is a member of the Korean Expatriate Literary Association.